Flying a Round

88 rounds and partner songs

chosen by David Gadsby and Beatrice Harrop
with an introduction and notes by John Bannister
and drawings by Bernard Cheese
and music performed by Vivien Ellis, Kirsty Hoiles, Sam Kenyon,
Missak Takoushian and Stephen Chadwick

D1475994

A & C Black · London

Second edition 2002
A & C Black Publishers Ltd, 37 Soho Square London W1D 3QZ
©2002, 1982 A & C Black Publishers Ltd
ISBN 0 7136 6343 X

Printed in Great Britain by Martins the Printers, Berwick upon Tweed

A & C Black uses paper produced with elemental chlorine-free pulp, harvested from managed sustainable forests.

Some of the rounds in this book (nos. 1, 7, 23, 52, 55, 56, 66, 70 and 71) are reproduced by kind permission of SING FOR PLEASURE, a singing movement with a particular interest in music for young people. It holds singing days and choral events in different parts of the country and membership includes choirs as well as individuals. For information, write to:

Sing for Pleasure
Unit 10A
Nortonthorpe Mill
Wakefield Road
Scissett
Huddersfield
HD8 9LA
0800 0184 164

Contents

```
Flying around
[1 book, 1
compact disc] :
          J782.
              42
1478983
```

Revving up

On the runway

Taking off

Flying high

Aerobatics

Formation flying

Crash landing

Introduction

This book contains 88 rounds and partner songs. A round is a short song sung by a number of voices which overlap each other. Before you start to sing a round, it's important that everyone really knows the song. Also, while singing, you need to listen – both to keep in time and to enjoy the pattern made by the different voices. Partner songs are two, or more, songs which can be sung 'against' each other. Again it's very important to listen while singing.

In this book the easiest rounds come at the beginning. As the book progresses, the rounds become more difficult so that real skill is needed to sing those in the "Aerobatics" section. Building in this way from the simple to the more complex fosters skills of musicianship difficult to develop in any other way.

Listening is the basis of all musicianship. In a round everyone knows all the music: by gradually becoming more aware of the other parts, the singers become used to the sound of harmony and counterpoint, and they appreciate the value of rhythmic independence. They also learn the skill of making music as an ensemble without the need for laborious teaching or learning.

Rounds are relatively short and can soon be memorised. As a result those who are singing can readily keep 'in touch' with each other, by listening and by watching. The sense of 'standing on your own feet' in order to hold a part, and yet relying on others to do the same in order to appreciate the music as a whole, makes for music making of the highest order.

Teaching rounds

There are many ways of introducing rounds and it is good to vary the approach from one song to another. One principle, however, always applies – *everyone must know the song thoroughly before dividing into parts*.

The details of teaching will vary according to the experience and confidence of the teacher, the age and skill of the class, the difficulties of the particular round, and the availability of accompaniment. Teachers with little or no experience of teaching rounds may like to have a detailed method to follow. One such method is given below. It may also be helpful to consider the following general points:

1 Don't be in a rush to 'get into parts'.
2 Think of many ways of involving the children, getting them to sing short passages a number of times while you provide the rest of the song.
3 Try to make music continuously, only stopping to talk as a last resort. If the children have not sung rounds before, then more stopping and explaining will no doubt be needed.

4 Aim for continual success by not asking for the impossible and by presenting the song in such a way that it is always sung accurately.
5 At all times encourage light accurate singing and awareness of the beat/pulse. Never allow anyone to cover their ears or to feel that it is a competition to see who can sing loudest or finish first. If this begins to happen, be content with two parts.
6 As you become more experienced at leading rounds, you will find that you can start singing with each group in turn, jumping from part to part to give support when needed.
7 You will quickly build up a repertoire of rounds, so that in each session with the children you may be starting a new one, establishing a partly learnt one, and singing an old favourite.

One method in detail

Here is one way of teaching "Canoe song" (no. 19).

First session

1 Introduce the round by talking about Canadian Indians, showing a picture of a canoe, etc.
2 Sing the whole song through to the children, possibly with guitar accompaniment. Only one chord, D minor, is needed for this round.
3 Repeat the song immediately, going straight back to the beginning so that everyone hears how the join is made.
4 At the end of the song, continue to sing "Dip, dip and swing" over and over, getting the children to join in, preferably by gesture of face or hand without stopping the music.
5 Add a simple paddling movement with both arms (Canadian Indian canoes have a single bladed paddle) still singing "Dip, dip and swing".
6 Sing the whole song through once or twice again while the children continue paddling and singing "Dip, dip and swing".
7 Stop the children with a hand sign (no more movement) while going straight back to the beginning and proceeding as follows, keeping the beat going and starting and stopping the children by signs:

Teacher: My paddle's keen and bright
Class: My paddle's keen and bright
(repeat the two phrases if needed)

Teacher: Flashing with silver
Class: Flashing with silver
(this section will almost certainly need repeating with suitable encouragement for posture and breathing, all done without stopping if possible)

Teacher: My paddle's keen and bright, flashing with silver
Class: My paddle's keen and bright, flashing with silver
Teacher: Follow the wild goose flight
Class: Follow the wild goose flight
Teacher: Dip, dip and swing
Class: Dip, dip and swing
Teacher: Follow the wild goose flight, dip, dip and swing
Class: Follow the wild goose flight, dip, dip and swing
Teacher: sings whole song
Class: repeats with teacher.

8 Repeat the song immediately, the class singing through to the end while the teacher drops out and goes back to singing "Dip, dip and swing" with paddle movement.
9 Still singing "Dip, dip and swing", get half the class to do the same, then start the other half singing the song through, probably twice.
10 The two groups reverse roles.
11 Stop to organise instrumental accompaniment (see **Accompaniment** section), then repeat steps 9 and 10 with accompaniment.

Apart from steps 1 and 11, this session should take little more than ten minutes.

Second session (preferably next day)
12 Revise the first session as needed until each half of the class can sing the melody confidently without support from the teacher. It's often useful to let each group listen to the other and suggest any improvements.
13 The class sings the song through twice, the teacher providing the second part by coming in as the class reaches the beginning of the second bar.
14 Repeat step 13 with each half of the class, if needed.
15 The class sings in two parts, one half starting and the other half coming in one bar later.
16 Repeat with the other half leading.
17 Add accompaniment if desired.

Third session
18 Revise singing in two parts.
19 Proceed in similar fashion until four parts are achieved.

Fourth session
20 Devise a little "Scena" in which the Indians are heard approaching from the distance, singing "Canoe song" as they paddle along the river. They make their camp, build their fire, sing "Land of the silver birch" (no. 49)

and any other Indian songs they know, then repeat "Canoe song" as they paddle away.

The words "Follow the wild goose flight" can be linked to the study of the Indians' north/south migrations and the geography and climate of North America.

Accompaniment
A simple accompaniment can be most valuable whilst a round is being learnt and before it is sung in parts. The learning or 'composing' of an accompaniment and the perfecting of its playing gives an invaluable 'excuse' for the many repetitions of the song that are necessary for it to be thoroughly learnt before it is sung in parts. In performance, rounds are generally best unaccompanied. The overlapping parts provide complete harmony and a satisfying rhythm. Unless the round really seems to need an accompaniment, it should be regarded as a prop to be discarded when the singers are sufficiently able and competent.

1 **Rhythm** A tight rhythmic pulse, or a repeated pattern, played on an unpitched instrument by the teacher is often a useful way of keeping a steadying hand on the over-enthusiastic.

2 **Ostinati** An ostinato is a repeated musical pattern. Ostinati are useful as an introduction to part singing and as a means of keeping everyone busy. They can sometimes make an interesting extra part to the round.
   Many of the rounds in this book have ostinati and others can easily be devised. Often the first or last line of a song can be used in this way, as in "Canoe song". A 'soh-doh' pattern usually works well with a one-chord round, e.g. "Shalom" (no. 44).

Where there are two or more chords, the root of each chord will make a good ostinato, e.g. "Calypso" (no. 68) can have the notes D G A D, each lasting for one bar. If these are played on an instrument at bass pitch, such as bass xylophone, piano, bass strings of guitar, open strings of cello or violin, the harmony will be supported without interfering with the melody. They can also be sung by a low voice.

3   **Chords** All rounds have a short chord sequence which is repeated at regular intervals. This makes chordal accompaniment easy. For quick reference, chords are listed for most of the songs. Like all suggestions for accompaniment, they are an optional extra.

(a) *Guitar* You don't need an enormous repertoire of chords. A capo will help you play in the key which best suits the voices. Guitar chords and suggestions for the use of a capo where useful are given with the songs. You can buy a capo cheaply from any guitar shop, or you can improvise one with a pencil and elastic band.

   Children can provide guitar chord accompaniment. If you have a number of guitars, you can teach one chord to each pupil, or pre-tune one guitar to each chord so that it only has to be strummed at the appropriate moment. Some rounds, of course, need only one chord.

(b) *Piano* A simple chordal accompaniment is usually better than an elaborate part which includes the melody line. "Let us endeavour" (no. 8), for example, can have the following accompaniment:

Repeat throughout

Children can play accompaniments of this kind, beginning with the bass notes only, then taking one 'hand' each.

(c) *Autoharp* Don't just strum across the whole instrument all the time. Experiment with low notes at the beginning of each bar and higher ones for the 'fill-in'.

(d) *Chime bars* Lay out your chime bars for each chord in order. For example, "Baby sardine" (no. 52) has two chords, D and A7. The notes in each chord are listed as D, F sharp, A; and A, E, G, A. Lay these out on two tables.

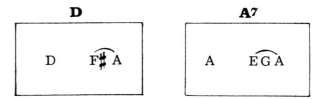

Play them together as a chord, as indicated in the song. Then split them up, playing the lowest note on its own followed by the rest of the chord in an 'um chick chick' pattern.

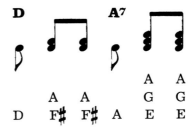

   You can do this entirely on your own, or you can employ up to seven children, one for each chime bar.

Finished performance
Don't be content with just 'singing it through'. Use ostinati, instrumental parts, recorders, etc. to play an introduction and coda, or interlude, as necessary. Plan how the round will be brought to an end. Record the finished product on tape sometimes, so that the singers can hear what it really sounds like. Above all, experiment and have a good time.

1 Algy

1 Al - gy met a bear, ——— The

2 bear met Al - gy. The

3 bear grew bul - gy The

4 bulge was Al - gy.

Words: traditional
Music: Pat Shaw

Ostinato

Piano or xylophones (bass can be omitted)

The figures 1 2 3 4 at the beginning of each line of music show that this round can be sung in up to four parts. Each new part starts two bars after the previous one. Even if only two (or three) groups or voices take part, each new part starts two bars after the previous one.

The ostinato for piano or xylophones can be used to accompany unison singing, and also as an introduction to the round, which might then be sung unaccompanied.

2 Music is fun

Mu - sic is fun.

Rum - tum - ty tum.

Sing - ing and play - ing will

nev - er be done!

Words: Kate Baxter
Music: traditional

Guitarists have a speedy change from the D7 chord to the G chord in the middle of each line.

The ostinati below offer easier alternatives for accompaniment.

Guitar chords

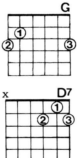

Ostinati
These ostinati can be played singly or together on chime bars, glockenspiel, piano, etc.

3 Lady, come down and see

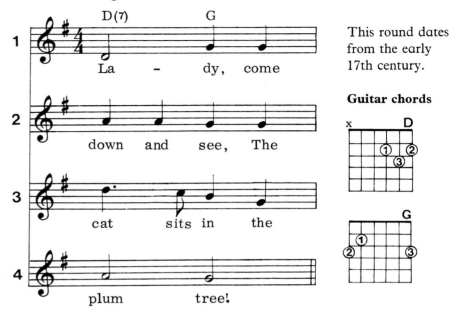

La - dy, come

down and see, The

cat sits in the

plum tree!

Words and music: traditional

This round dates from the early 17th century.

Guitar chords

Ostinato
This ostinato is probably best played on a bass instrument.

Chords
Piano, autoharp or chime bars accompaniments can be built up on the following chords (see Introduction)

D	G			D		G	
A							
F♯	B						
D	G		e.g. D	F♯	A	G	B

4 A thousand hairy savages

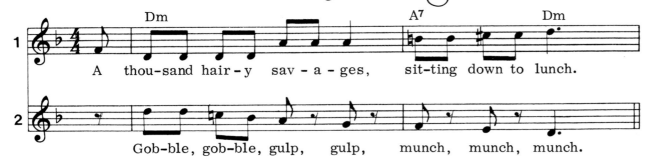

1. A thou-sand hair-y sav-a-ges, sit-ting down to lunch.

2. Gob-ble, gob-ble, gulp, gulp, munch, munch, munch.

Words: Spike Milligan
Music: Ken Lee

Guitar chords

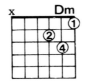

Ostinato

The ostinato can be sung softly or played. A bass xylophone would be a good instrument to use.

One thou - sand sa - va - ges, one thou - sand sa - va - ges

Chords for instrumental accompaniment

Dm	**A**⁷
A	A
F	G
D	C♯

e.g. D F A D F A C♯ G A D F A

5 White swans

Guitar chord

Words: Kenneth Simpson
Music: traditional

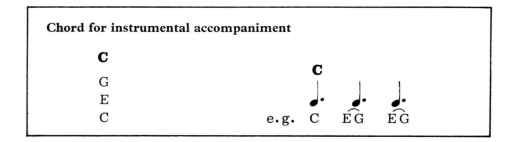

Chord for instrumental accompaniment

6 Cuckoo's gone away

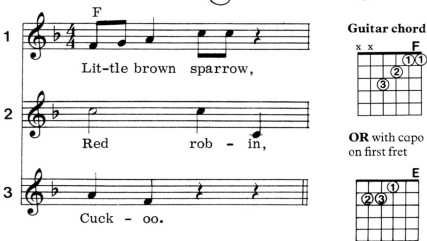

Guitar chord

OR with capo on first fret

Words and music: Jan Holdstock

This song can be sung by three groups, each taking one bird call only. The first group starts, then the second group joins in, and then the third group, and all go on singing their call to make a "bird chorus". The song can also be sung as a round, each voice or group repeating all the calls in turn.

Instruments can play in the three rests to keep the time going,

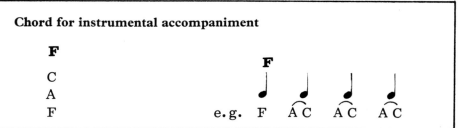

7 Lollipop man

1. When I grow up
2. I'd like to be
3. A lol-li-pop man
4. 'Cos they don't start work
5. Till they're six - ty.

Words and music: John Coates

Try singing this song in two parts to begin with – it's not necessary to have all five, but it's much more fun!

Guitar chords

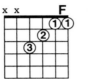 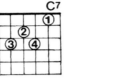

Guitarists may prefer to play chords E and B7 with capo on first fret.

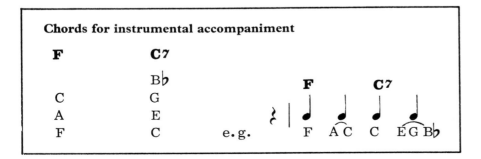

Chords for instrumental accompaniment

F	C7
	Bb
C	G
A	E
F	C

e.g. F (FAC) C7 (EGBb)

8 Let us endeavour

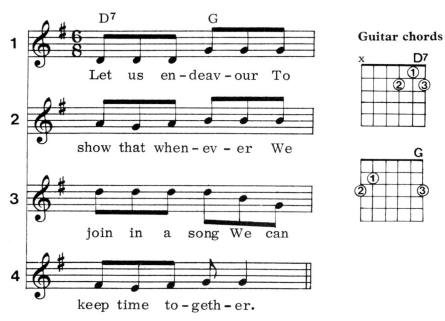

1 Let us en-deav-our To

2 show that when-ev-er We

3 join in a song We can

4 keep time to-geth-er.

Words and music: anonymous

Guitar chords

Ostinato

With a swing

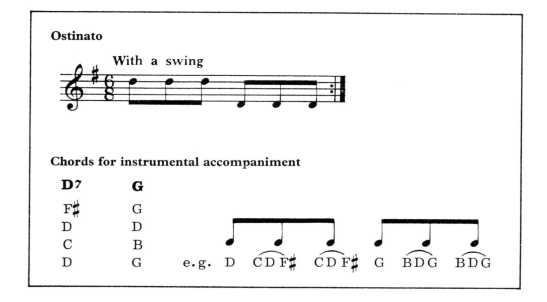

Chords for instrumental accompaniment

D⁷	G	
F♯	G	
D	G	
C	B	
D	G	e.g. D CD F♯ CD F♯ G BDG BDG

9 Make new friends

1 Make new friends, but

2 keep the old.

3 One is sil-ver and the

4 oth-er gold.

Words and music: traditional

Ostinato

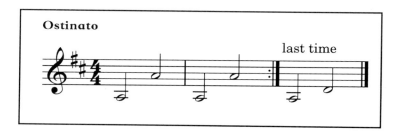

last time

Guitar chords

The guitar chords
must be used only
for unison singing.

10 Something inside me

G   D

1 Some-thing in-side me says,

2 "Time for my tea,

3 Time for my tea,

4 Time for my tea!"

Words and music: Kenneth Simpson

Guitar chords

G

x   D

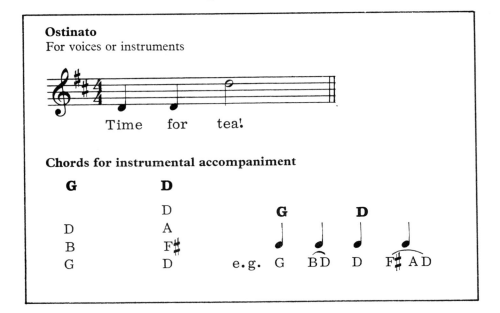

Ostinato
For voices or instruments

Time for tea!

Chords for instrumental accompaniment

G	**D**		
	D	**G**	**D**
D	A		
B	F♯		
G	D	e.g. G B͡D	D F♯ A͡D

11 Why shouldn't my goose ?

1. Why should-n't my goose
2. Lay as well as thy goose
3. When I paid for my goose
4. Twice as much as thou?

Words and music: traditional

Guitar chord

Guitarists may like to tune the 6th string down to D, to give a six-string D chord with a strong bass.

12 Donkeys and carrots

1. Don-keys are in love with car-rots,
2. Car-rots aren't in love at all.
3. Hee - haw, hee - haw,
4. Lis - ten to that lov - ing call!

Words: English paraphrase by Augustus D. Zanzig
Music: traditional Belgian

PARTNER SONGS

As well as being sung as rounds, the two songs on this page can be sung together as partner songs, one group singing "Why shouldn't my goose ?" while a second group is singing "Donkeys and carrots" (track 12a).

If the pitch is too low, the songs can be sung in E flat (guitarists play chord D with capo on first fret) or in E.

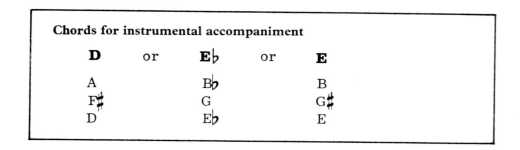

Chords for instrumental accompaniment

D	or	E♭	or	E
A		B♭		B
F♯		G		G♯
D		E♭		E

Ostinato
This bass ostinato can be used with both rounds.

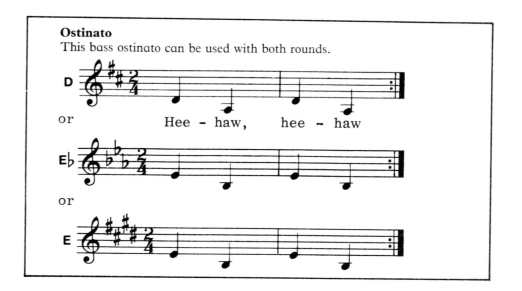

D

or Hee - haw, hee - haw

E♭

or

E

13 Sing this song

Sing this song
whilst you play.
Sing it in the eve-ning and at
break of day.

Words: Michael Jessett, adapted by John Bannister
Music: traditional

Ostinato
This ostinato is best played on a bass instrument.

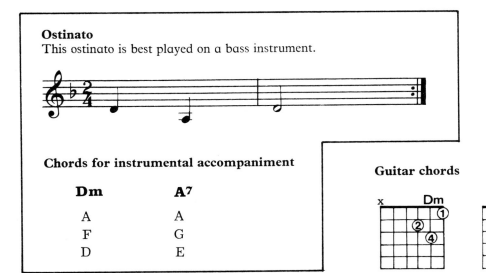

Chords for instrumental accompaniment

Dm	A⁷
A	A
F	G
D	E

14 Hey ho! Time to go to bed

Hey, ho! time to go to bed.
Why can't I feel just as wide a-wake
When it's time to get up in the morning?

Words: Beatrice Harrop
Music: traditional

Ostinato

Guitar chords

15 Softly sings the donkey

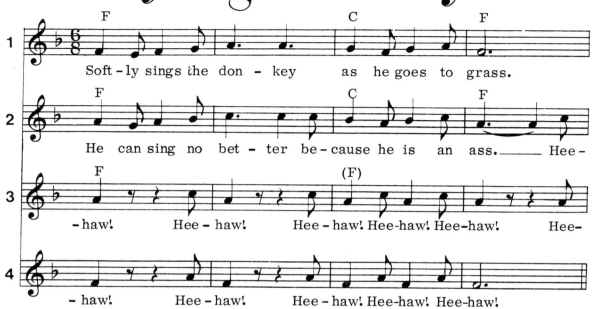

1. Soft-ly sings the don-key as he goes to grass.
2. He can sing no bet-ter be-cause he is an ass.——— Hee-
3. -haw! Hee-haw! Hee-haw! Hee-haw! Hee-haw! Hee-
4. -haw! Hee-haw! Hee-haw! Hee-haw! Hee-haw!

Words and music: traditional

Guitar chords for songs 15 and 16

OR with capo on first fret

Guitarists can play chords E and B7 with capo on the first fret. Another alternative is to play chords F and C, tuning the sixth string up to F for extra bass.

When the song is sung as a round, both chords happen at once in the third bar, making a special "hee-haw" effect, which is probably best left to voices unaccompanied.

Chords for instrumental accompaniment	
F	**C**
C	G
A	E
F	C

16 Kite flying high

1. Kite fly-ing high in the blue of the sky.

2. Pull, pull and tug it goes, pull, pull and tug it goes,

3. Pull, pull and tug it goes, soar-ing on high.

Words: Beatrice Harrop
Music: traditional German

Guitarists can play chords E and B7 with capo on the first fret.

Aim for a smooth singing line with a good swing so that the music soars like the kite.

Ostinato

The ostinato is suitable for voices or instruments. It can be played on the piano an octave lower.

Oh, look at my fine kite!

Chords for instrumental accompaniment

F	**C**
C	G
A	E
F	C

17 'Morning, Mr Blackbird

'Morn - ing, Mis - ter Black - bird,

How's your wife and fa - mi - ly?

Sto - len by a mag - pie and

tak - en for his tea.

Words and music: Jo Gadsby

The composer of this round had discovered a blackbird's nest with eggs in it. When she went along later, the eggs had disappeared and magpies had been seen around.

Guitar chord

Ostinato
This ostinato would be most effective played on a bass instrument.

last time

18 Thirty purple birds

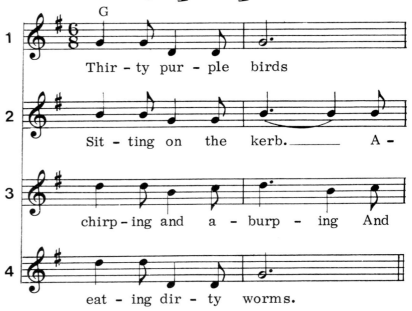

Thir - ty pur - ple birds

Sit - ting on the kerb. _____ A -

chirp - ing and a - burp - ing And

eat - ing dir - ty worms.

Words: anonymous
Music: Beatrice Harrop

Singers might like to sing the words of this round in the original New York dialect as given below:

> Toity poiple boids
> Sitt'n on der coib
> A-choipin' and a-boipin'
> An' eat'n doity woims.

Untuned percussion instruments can be used to give sound effects.

Chord for instruments

G

D

B

G

Guitar chord

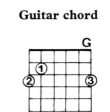

19 Canoe song

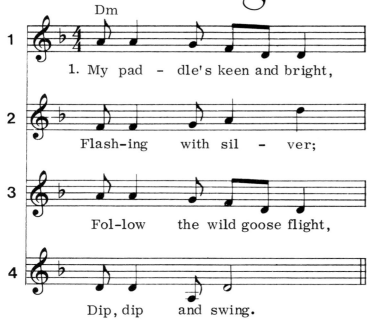

1. My pad - dle's keen and bright,

Flash-ing with sil - ver;

Fol-low the wild goose flight,

Dip, dip and swing.

2 Dip, dip and swing her back,
Flashing with silver;
Follow the wild goose flight,
Dip, dip and swing.

Words and music: Margaret Embers McGee

Guitarists can tune the bass string down to D to give extra bass.

This song can be sung as a partner song to "Land of the silver birch" (no. 49), or the two songs can be linked by using the same ostinato for both (track 49a).

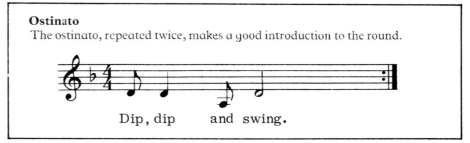

Ostinato
The ostinato, repeated twice, makes a good introduction to the round.

Dip, dip and swing.

Detailed notes on the teaching and follow-up of this round are given in the introduction to the book.

If a slightly higher pitch is needed, the song can be sung in E minor.

Guitar chord

Chords for instrumental accompaniment		
Dm	or	**Em**
A		B
F		G
D		E

20 Trav'lin' round

1. Trav' - lin' and a - trav' - lin' and a -
2. trav' - lin' a - long. And
3. all the time we're trav' - lin' we're a -
4. sing - in' a song.

Words and music: Ralph Alan Dale

21 Song of the frogs

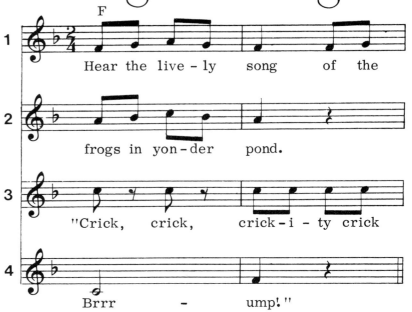

1. Hear the live - ly song of the
2. frogs in yon - der pond.
3. "Crick, crick, crick - i - ty crick
4. Brrr - ump!"

Words and music: anonymous

Guitar chord

  F

OR
with capo
on first fret

  E

Guitarists can play chord E with capo on first fret.

Guitarists can play chord E with capo on first fret.

Percussion or mouth music
For use while the song is sung in unison

3/4 ch ch ch ch ch ch

Chord for instruments
The same chord is used for both rounds.

F

C
A
F

Ostinato
For use while the song is sung in unison

Guiro 2/4

Drum 2/4

"Brrr - ump!"

22 Frogs' festival

1 This is the day for the

2 frogs by the pond,

3 Feast-ing and sing-ing and

4 danc-ing a - round.

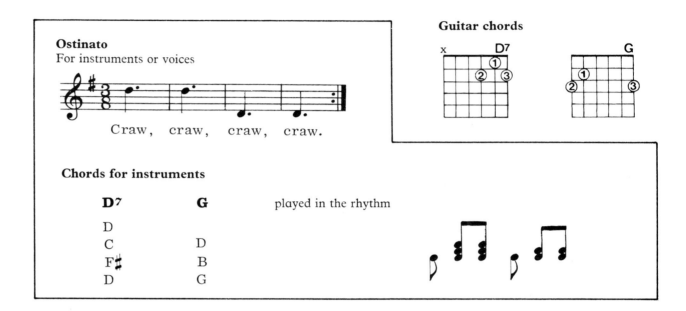

Ostinato
For instruments or voices

Craw, craw, craw, craw.

Chords for instruments

D⁷	G	played in the rhythm
D		
C	D	
F♯	B	
D	G	

Guitar chords

x   D7   G

Words: translated from the German by Mabel F. Wilson
Music: traditional German

This round is for four voices or groups, each part coming in two bars after the previous one.

23 Nice but naughty thoughts

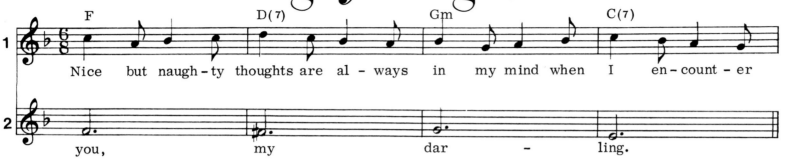

Nice but naugh-ty thoughts are al-ways in my mind when I en-count-er

you, my dar - ling.

Words and music: John Coates

Guitarists may prefer to pitch the song a tone higher and play chords G E(7) Am D(7). See opposite page for chord diagrams.

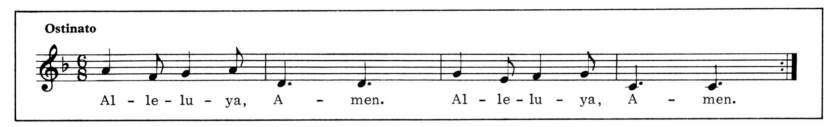

Ostinato

Al - le - lu - ya, A - men. Al - le - lu - ya, A - men.

Chords for instruments

F	D7	Gm	C7
C	C	D	Bb
A	F#	Bb	E
F	D	G	C

24 Sandy McNab

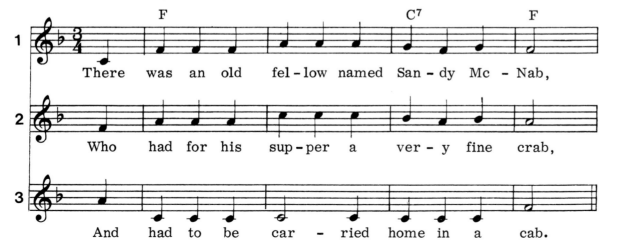

There was an old fel-low named San-dy Mc-Nab,

Who had for his sup-per a ver-y fine crab,

And had to be car - ried home in a cab.

Words and music: traditional Scottish

Guitarists can play chords E and B7 with capo on first fret. See opposite page for chord diagrams.

Chords for instrumental accompaniment

F	C7
	(C)
C	Bb
A	E
F	C

25 Ticking clocks

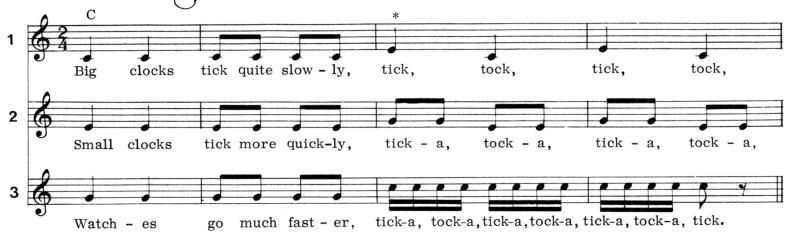

Guitar chord

1. Big clocks tick quite slow-ly, tick, tock, tick, tock,

2. Small clocks tick more quick-ly, tick - a, tock - a, tick - a, tock - a,

3. Watch - es go much fast - er, tick-a, tock-a, tick-a, tock-a, tick-a, tock-a, tick.

Words: English adaptation by Beatrice Harrop
Music: traditional Danish

If desired this round can be sung in six parts, each new part coming in two bars after the previous part (see *)

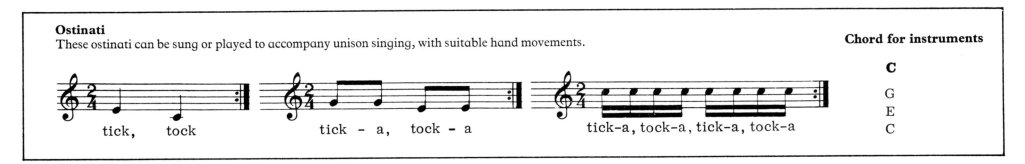

Ostinati
These ostinati can be sung or played to accompany unison singing, with suitable hand movements.

Chord for instruments

C
G
E
C

tick, tock   tick - a, tock - a   tick-a, tock-a, tick-a, tock-a

Guitar chords for songs 23 and 24 (arranged alphabetically)

26 Water wagtail

Wa - ter, wa - ter wag - tail,

How ma-ny chil - dren have you?

Two a - sleep,____ two with the sheep,

Two to thresh the corn ears.

Words: Olwen Clark, written when she was six years old
Music: J.S.

Guitar chords

Dm   A7

Chords for instruments	
Dm	**A7**
	A
A	G
F	E
D	C#

27 Row the boat

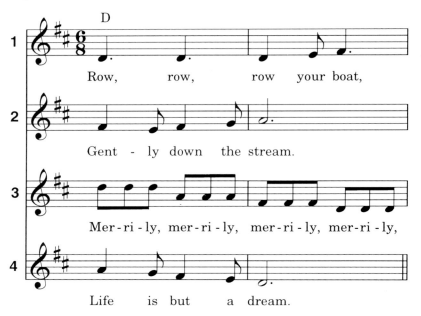

Row, row, row your boat,

Gent - ly down the stream.

Mer - ri - ly, mer-ri - ly, mer-ri - ly, mer-ri - ly,

Life is but a dream.

Words and music: traditional

Guitar chord

Chord for instruments
D
D
A
F#
D

28 On the river flows

1. On the riv-er flows, strong, deep and si - lent.

2. On the riv-er flows, strong, deep and si - lent.

3. On to the might - y o - cean,

4. On to the might - y o - cean.

Words: Chris Green
Music: traditional

This round needs no accompaniment. A full, rich sound is needed like the strong flow of the river.

29 Kookaburra

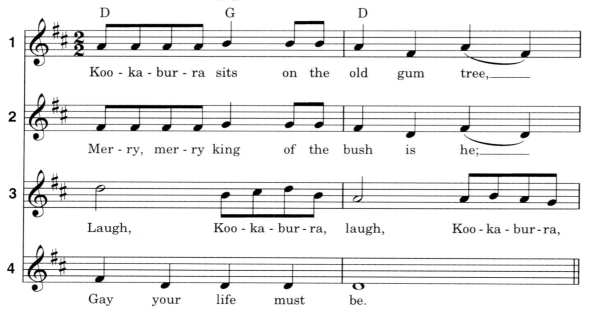

1. Koo - ka - bur - ra sits on the old gum tree,_____
2. Mer - ry, mer - ry king of the bush is he;_____
3. Laugh, Koo - ka - bur - ra, laugh, Koo - ka - bur - ra,
4. Gay your life must be.

Words and music: traditional Australian

The kookaburra is a bird native to Australia. It has a gurgling call which makes it sound as if it is laughing and it is sometimes called a laughing jackass. It is a bird of the kingfisher family with brown plumage.

Ostinato

The ostinato can be played by three recorders, or it can be sung by three voices (sing the treble recorder part an octave lower than written!)

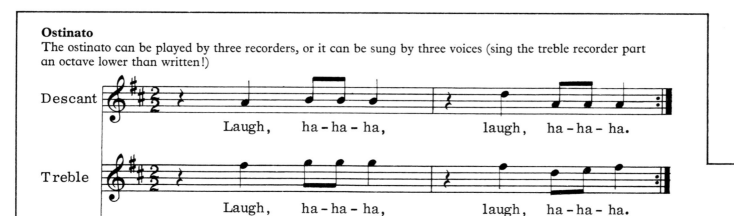

Descant: Laugh, ha - ha - ha, laugh, ha - ha - ha.

Treble: Laugh, ha - ha - ha, laugh, ha - ha - ha.

Tenor: Laugh with me!_____

Guitar chords

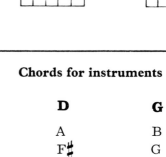

Chords for instruments

D	G
A	B
F#	G
D	D

30 Brown and yellow keskidee

1. Brown and yel - low kes - ki - dee,
2. Sit - ting in a ban - yan tree,
3. Chirp - ing there so mer - ri - ly,
4. Do come down and play with me.

Words and music: anonymous

The keskidee is a bird native to Trinidad. It has a strange call which sounds as if it is saying "Qu'est-ce qu'il dit?", the French for "What does he say?", hence its name.

Ostinato

The ostinato, imitating chirping, can be played on a glockenspiel, or other high-pitched instrument.

Chords for instruments

D	A⁷
D	C♯
A	A
F♯	G
D	A

Guitar chords

31 Derry ding ding dason

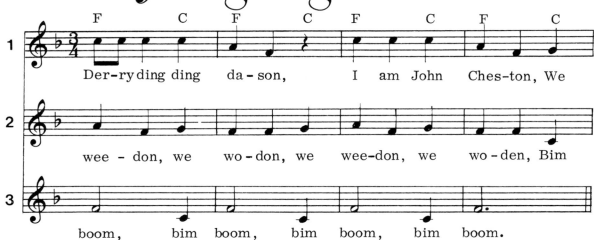

Words and music: traditional

This is an old weaving song, sung to the rhythm of the clattering looms. It is marked for singing as a three-part round. Once everyone is confident and singing rhythmically, it can be sung in up to twelve parts, each part coming in one bar after the previous one.

32 Sing, sing together

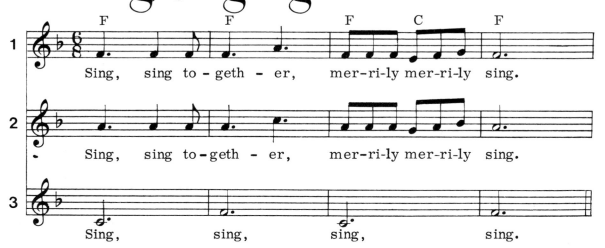

Words and music: traditional

Guitarists may prefer to play chords E and B7 with capo on first fret.

Chords for instruments

F	C
C	C
A	G
F	E

Guitarists can play chords E and B7 with capo on first fret.

Guitar chords

OR with capo on first fret

33 Clap, stamp, slap, click

1 First you make your fin-gers click,

2 Then you stamp your feet.

3 Both hands slap your knees and

4 clap on the beat.

Words and music: Jan Holdstock

Make the appropriate action at each * as the word is sung. This round can also have an action ostinato as given below.

Guitar chord

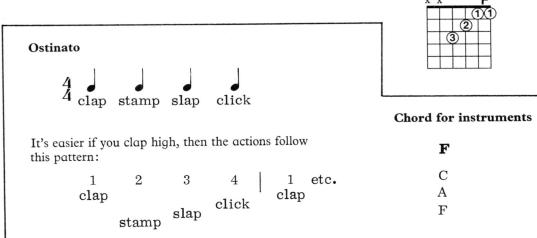

Ostinato

4/4   clap   stamp   slap   click

It's easier if you clap high, then the actions follow this pattern:

1	2	3	4		1	etc.
clap					clap	
	stamp					
		slap				
			click			

Chord for instruments

F
C
A
F

34 Frère Jacques

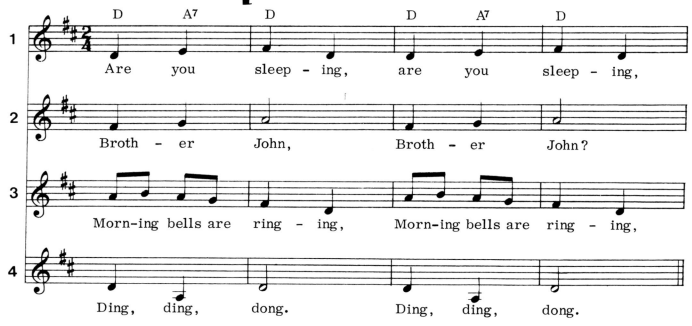

1 Are you sleep - ing, are you sleep - ing,

2 Broth - er John, Broth - er John?

3 Morn-ing bells are ring - ing, Morn-ing bells are ring - ing,

4 Ding, ding, dong. Ding, ding, dong.

Words and music: from the traditional French

Here are the French words of this round:
Frère Jacques, Frère Jacques,
Dormez-vous, dormez-vous ?
Sonnez les matines, sonnez les matines,
Dinn, din, don. Dinn, din, don.

PARTNER SONGS

The two rounds "Frère Jacques" and "Three blind mice" can be sung together as partner songs.

The ostinato fits both rounds and can be used also when the songs are sung together (track 35a).

Ostinato
Chime bars are suitable

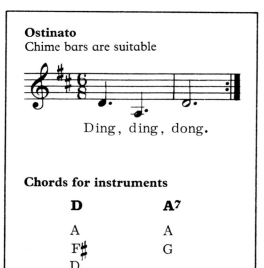

Ding, ding, dong.

Chords for instruments

D	**A⁷**
A	A
F#	G
D	

Guitar chords

35 Three blind mice

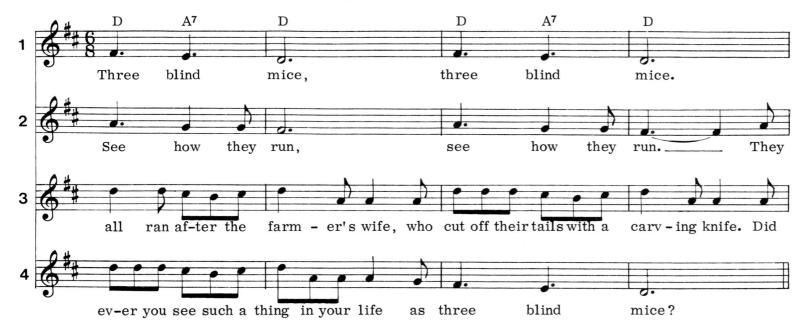

Three blind mice, three blind mice.

See how they run, see how they run. _____ They

all ran af-ter the farm - er's wife, who cut off their tails with a carv - ing knife. Did

ev-er you see such a thing in your life as three blind mice?

Words and music: traditional

36 Man's life's a vapour

1. Man's life's a va-pour full of woes.
2. He cuts a ca-per, down he goes.
3. Down he, down he, down he, down he, down he goes.

Words and music: traditional

Guitarists can play chords E and B7 with capo on first fret.

Chords for instruments

F	C7
	B♭
C	G
A	E
F	C

Guitar chords for songs 36 and 37

Song 36

F   C7

OR with capo on first fret

E   B7

Song 37

Dm

A7

37 Hodge's grace

O Heaven-ly Fa - ther, bless us

And keep us all a - live.

There's ten of us for din - ner

And not e - nough for five.

Words: anonymous
Music: Beatrice Harrop

Sing this round quietly as a prayer.

Ostinato
This ostinato is best played on a bass instrument.

38 Hard fact

One two three four five six seven,

All good chil - dren go to heaven.

That's why there are so ve - ry

few on earth.

Words and music: Jan Holdstock

This round is best sung unaccompanied.

Notice the unusual time signature of seven crotchet beats in the bar.

39 Here lie the bones

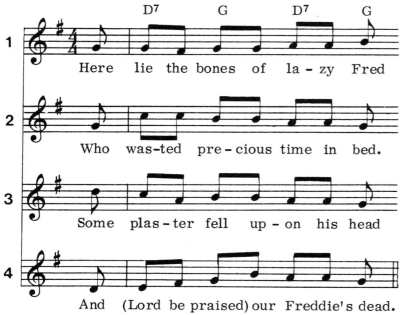

Here lie the bones of la-zy Fred

Who was-ted pre-cious time in bed.

Some plas-ter fell up-on his head

And (Lord be praised) our Freddie's dead.

Words: adapted from a 19th century tombstone
Music: Thomas Tallis

Try singing this round slowly and solemnly like the original hymn tune.
Try singing it fast and mischievously, too.

Ostinato
Play this on a bass instrument (sustained, if possible).

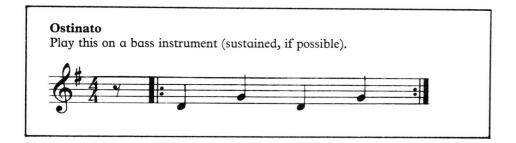

40 Blow the wind southerly

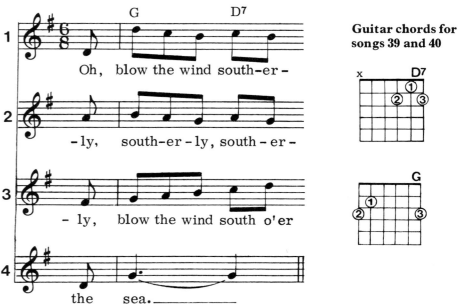

Oh, blow the wind south-er-

-ly, south-er-ly, south-er-

-ly, blow the wind south o'er

the sea.

Words and music: Imogen Holst

Guitar chords for songs 39 and 40

Ostinato
last time

Blow, blow the wind.

Chords for instruments

G	D7
	D
D	C
B	A
G	D

41 Bellringer, pray give us some peace

Bell - ring - er, pray give us some peace.

Will your per - for - mance nev - er cease?

Wa-king us at dawn with the sound of your ring - ing,

Nev - er stop -ping once till the end of the day.

Bell - ring - er, when will your arms be worn a - way?

Bell - ring - er, when will your arms be worn a - way?

Words: Chris Green   Music: traditional

Guitarists can play chords E and B7 with capo on first fret.

Guitar chords

OR with capo on first fret

Whilst the song is sung in unison, the ostinato and the chords played by chime bars will help to create the clatter of the bells. When the round is sung in parts, chime bars players can provide an introduction and then join in the singing.

Ostinato

Chords for chime bars

F	C(7)
	(B♭)
C	G
A	E
F	C

42 Old Abram Brown

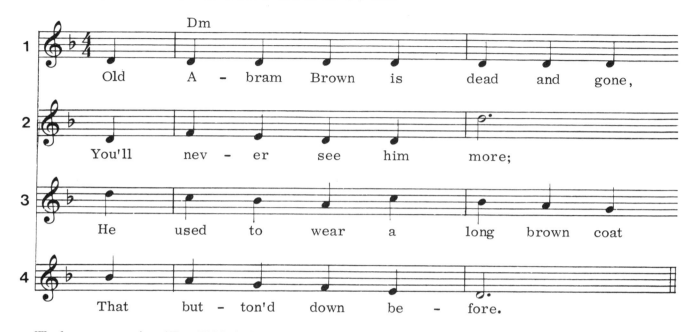

1. Old A-bram Brown is dead and gone,
2. You'll nev-er see him more;
3. He used to wear a long brown coat
4. That but-ton'd down be-fore.

Words: anonymous from 'Tom Tiddler's Ground'
Music: Benjamin Britten

Be sure to take a deep breath after "gone" so as to be able to rise to "more" at the end of the next line with confidence.

Care must be taken with the descending phrases or they will go flat.

Chime bars ringing out top and bottom D at the beginning of each bar will create the effect of the "passing bell" and will also help intonation.

Guitarists can tune the bass string down to D to give a six-string D minor chord with rich bass.

Guitar chord

This tune can be sung at half speed, and double speed, or in any combination.

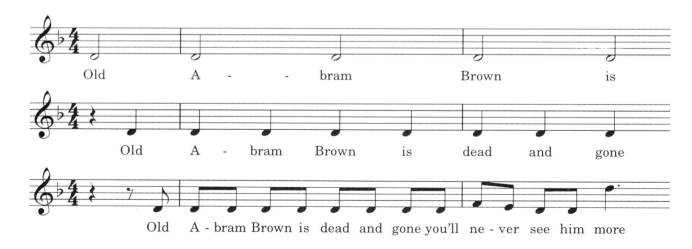

Old A - - bram Brown is

Old A - bram Brown is dead and gone

Old A - bram Brown is dead and gone you'll ne - ver see him more

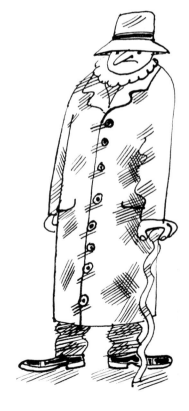

43 I like the flowers

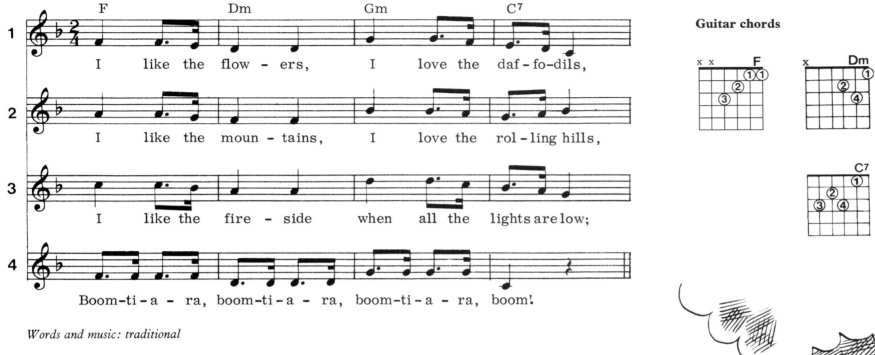

Words and music: traditional

Chords for instruments

F	Dm	Gm	C⁷
			B♭
C	A	G	G
A	F	D	E
F	D	B♭	C

44 Shalom

Sha - lom, my friend, sha - lom, my friend,

Sha - lom, sha - lom.

Un - til we meet a - gain, my friend,

Sha - lom, sha - lom.

Words and music: from the traditional Hebrew

Guitarists may like to tune the sixth string down to D to give a six-string D minor chord with rich bass.

Guitar chord

Ostinato
For voice or instrument

Sha - lom

Chords for instruments

Dm

A
F
D

45 Little wind

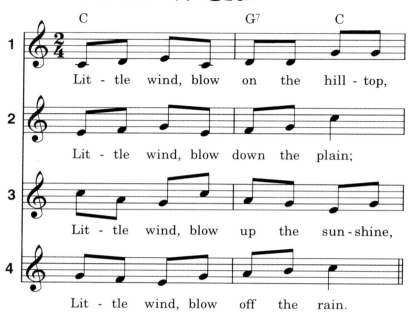

Lit - tle wind, blow on the hill - top,

Lit - tle wind, blow down the plain;

Lit - tle wind, blow up the sun - shine,

Lit - tle wind, blow off the rain.

Words: Kate Greenaway
Music: Deborah Burbridge

Guitar chords

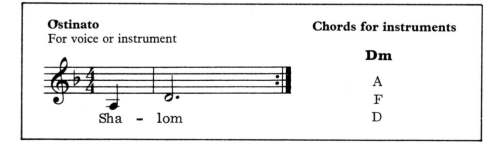

46 Come follow

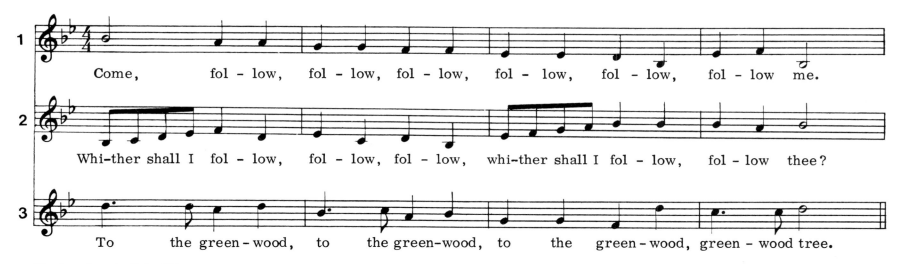

1. Come, fol - low, fol - low, fol - low, fol - low, fol - low, fol - low me.

2. Whi-ther shall I fol - low, fol - low, fol - low, whi-ther shall I fol - low, fol - low thee?

3. To the green - wood, to the green-wood, to the green - wood, green - wood tree.

Words and music: John Hilton

47 Gravity

Be - ware the force of Gra - vi - ty

Which draws the bread you have at tea

Straight to the ground,

But - ter side down.

Words and music: Jan Holdstock

Guitar chords

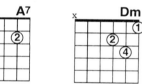

Ostinato
An ostinato for xylophones

Alto xylophone

Bass xylophone (don't play this at treble pitch!)

48 The cold old house

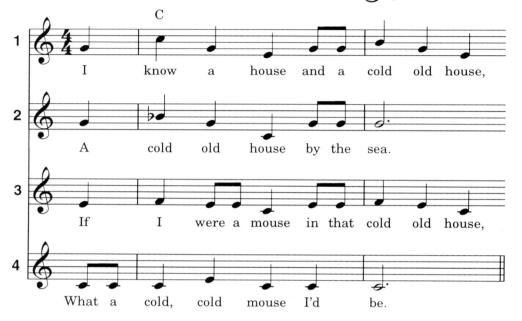

I know a house and a cold old house,

A cold old house by the sea.

If I were a mouse in that cold old house,

What a cold, cold mouse I'd be.

Words: anonymous
Music: Deborah Burbridge

Do not use the guitar accompaniment once the melody
has been learnt – it sounds too comfortable.

Guitar chord

Ostinato
An ostinato for glockenspiels

49 Land of the silver birch

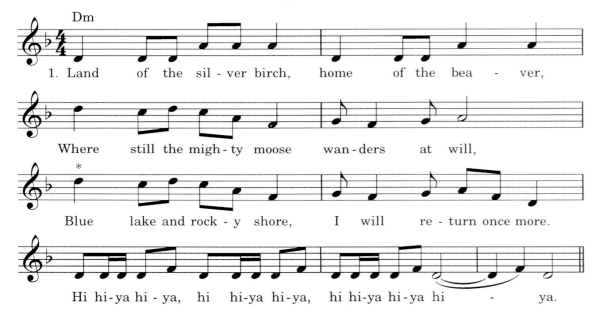

1. Land of the sil-ver birch, home of the bea-ver,

Where still the migh-ty moose wan-ders at will,

* Blue lake and rock-y shore, I will re-turn once more.

Hi hi-ya hi-ya, hi hi-ya hi-ya, hi hi-ya hi-ya hi - ya.

2 Down in the forest, deep in the lowlands,
My heart cries out for you, hills of the north.
Blue lake and rocky shore, I will return once more,
Hi hiya hiya, hi hiya hiya, hi hiya hiya hiya.

3 Swift as a silver fish, canoe of birch bark,
Thy mighty waterways carry me forth.
Blue lake and rocky shore, I will return once more,
Hi hiya hiya, hi hiya hiya, hi hiya hiya hiya.

4 There where the blue lake lies, I'll set my wigwam,
Close by the water's edge, silent and still.
Blue lake and rocky shore, I will return once more,
Hi hiya hiya, hi hiya, hiya, hi hiya hiya hiya.

Words and music: from a traditional Canadian Indian canoeing song

This song can be sung as a round in two parts, the second part beginning when the first part reaches the beginning of the third line (see *).

It can also be sung as a partner song with "Canoe song" (no. 19) (track 49a).

Ostinato
A tom-tom rhythm for drums

Chord for instruments

Dm

A
F
D

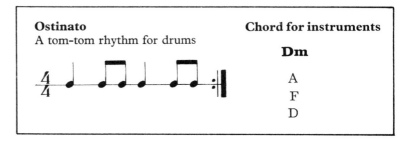

Guitar chord

Guitarists may like to tune the sixth string down to D to give a six-string D minor chord.

50 Poor fly

Lit - tle fly up - on the wall, Ain't you got no clothes at all?

Ain't you got no shim - my shirt? Ain't you got no pet - ti - skirt?

Don't you nev - er brush your hair? 'Tain't be - cause you've got no hair.

It's be - cause your mum don't care. Poor fly.

This song can be sung in two parts, the second part beginning when the first part reaches the beginning of the second line.

Words: anonymous
Music: Carey Blyton

Guitar chords

51 Old Jim John

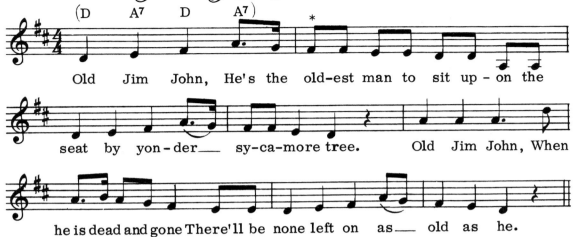

Old Jim John, He's the old-est man to sit up – on the
seat by yon-der__ sy-ca-more tree. Old Jim John, When
he is dead and gone There'll be none left on as__ old as he.

Words and music: Thomas Pitfield

This song can be sung as a two-part round, the second part beginning when the first part reaches the
beginning of the second bar (see *)

Guitar chords
The pattern given in brackets can be repeated
for each bar of the song.

Ostinato

52 Baby sardine

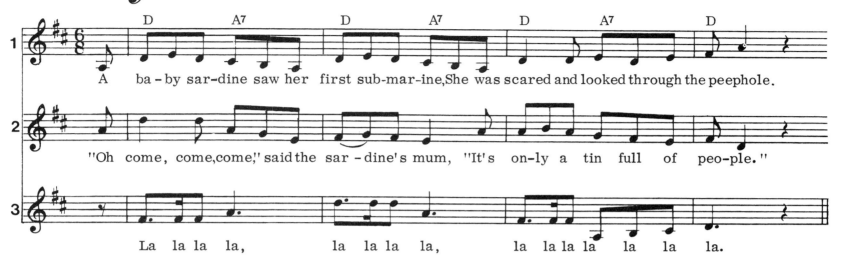

A ba-by sar-dine saw her first sub-mar-ine, She was scared and looked through the peephole.

"Oh come, come, come," said the sar-dine's mum, "It's on-ly a tin full of peo-ple."

La la la la, la la la la, la la la la la la la.

Words: Spike Milligan
Music: P. Wooding/J. Wild

Guitar chords

D

A7

If the pitch is too low, the song can be sung in E flat (guitarists play chords D and A7 with capo on first fret) or in E with chords E and B7.

OR

E

B7

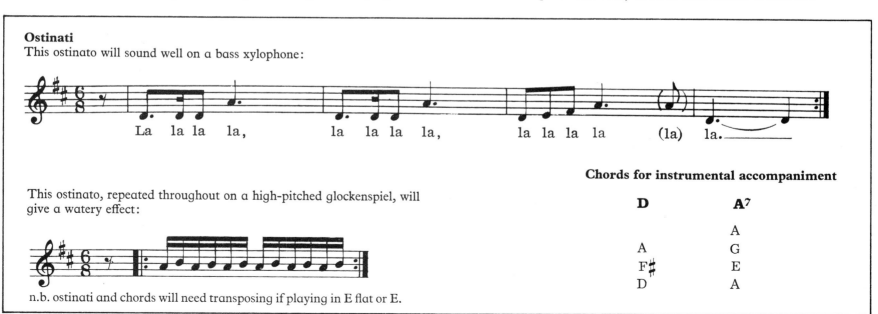

Ostinati
This ostinato will sound well on a bass xylophone:

La la la la, la la la la, la la la la (la) la.

This ostinato, repeated throughout on a high-pitched glockenspiel, will give a watery effect:

n.b. ostinati and chords will need transposing if playing in E flat or E.

Chords for instrumental accompaniment

D	A7
	A
A	G
F♯	E
D	A

53 Things that go bump in the night

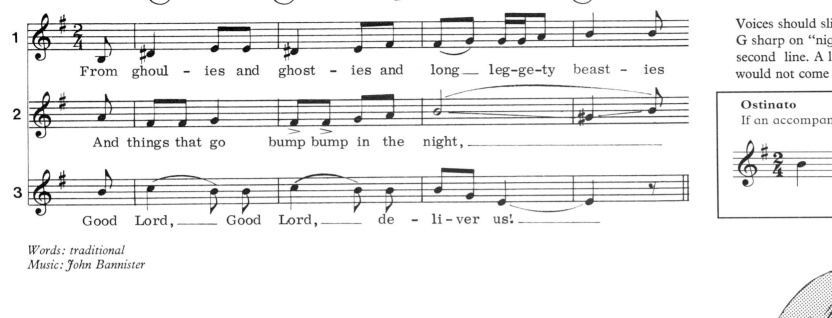

1. From ghoul - ies and ghost - ies and long___ leg-ge-ty beast - ies

2. And things that go bump bump in the night,_____

3. Good Lord,___ Good Lord,___ de - li-ver us!___

Words: traditional
Music: John Bannister

Voices should slide slowly to and from the G sharp on "night" at the end of the second line. A little tremble in the voice would not come amiss!

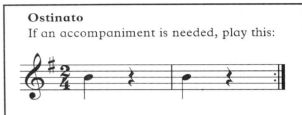

Ostinato

If an accompaniment is needed, play this:

54 The windmill

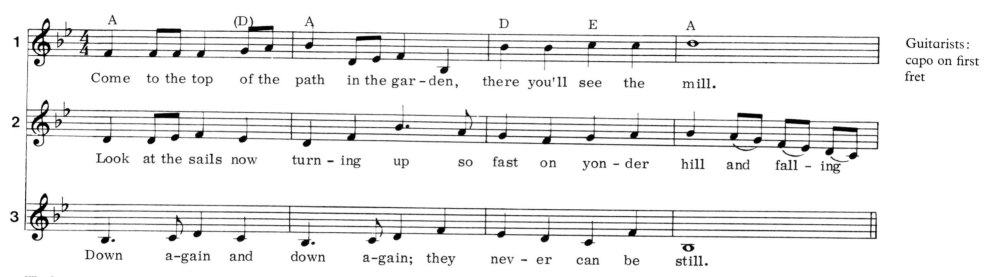

1 Come to the top of the path in the gar-den, there you'll see the mill.

2 Look at the sails now turn - ing up so fast on yon - der hill and fall - ing

3 Down a-gain and down a-gain; they nev - er can be still.

Guitarists: capo on first fret

Words: anonymous
Music: E. Nelham ("Slaves to the world")

Guitarists will need to place a capo on the first fret in order to play in the key of B flat as written.

Guitar chords
Capo on first fret

55 To stop the train

Words: *adapted from notice in trains*
Music: *P. Shaw/J. Wild*

Ostinato

Fif-ty pounds, fif-ty pounds

Chords for instruments

G	D⁷
	D
D	C
B	F♯
G	D

56 The duchess

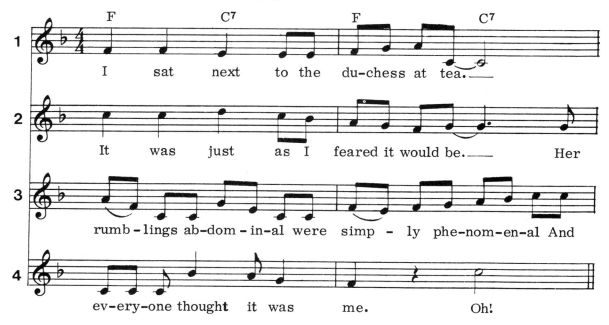

I sat next to the du-chess at tea.___

It was just as I feared it would be.___ Her

rumb-lings ab-dom-in-al were simp - ly phe-nom-en-al And

ev-ery-one thought it was me. Oh!

Words and music: Arthur Lucas

Guitarists may prefer to play chords E and B7 with capo on first fret.

Guitar chords

OR with capo on first fret

Chords for instruments	
F	**C7**
	C
C	B♭
A	G
F	C

57 The wreck

Un-der-neath the sea, Far a-way from land,

That's where I will be, Shak-ing on the sand,

Rat-tling in my rig-ging, Dith-ering on my deck, I'm just a

ner - - - vous wreck!

Words and music: Jan Holdstock

Take care that nobody sings in the rests. They help to give a nervous feel to the song.

In the last bar three creaking sounds can be made on beats 2, 3 and 4 to keep the beat going.

Guitar chords

Em

B7

Chords for instruments

Em	B7
	B
B	A
G	F♯
E	B

58 Let us sing together

Guitar chords

1. Let us sing to-geth-er, let us sing to-geth - er, One and all a joy - ous song.

2. Let us sing to - geth - er, One and all a joy - ous song.

3. Let us sing a - gain and a-gain, Let us sing a - gain and a-gain,

4. Let us sing a - gain and a-gain, One and all a joy - ous song.

Words and music: adapted from the Czech by Max V. Exner

Ostinato

Play on a bass instrument if possible.

59 Sound waves

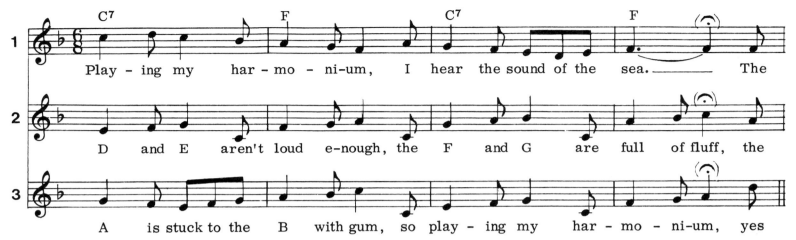

1. Play-ing my har-mo-ni-um, I hear the sound of the sea.____ The
2. D and E aren't loud e-nough, the F and G are full of fluff, the
3. A is stuck to the B with gum, so play-ing my har-mo-ni-um, yes

Words and music: Jan Holdstock

This round is best brought to an end at the points marked 𝄐 in the last bar of each line.

Guitarists can play chords B7 and E with capo on first fret.

Guitar chords

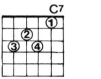

OR with capo on first fret

Ostinato

Melodicas would be very suitable for the ostinato and also for the chordal accompaniment.

Chords for instrumental accompaniment

C7	F
C	
Bb	C
G	A
C	F

60 Country life

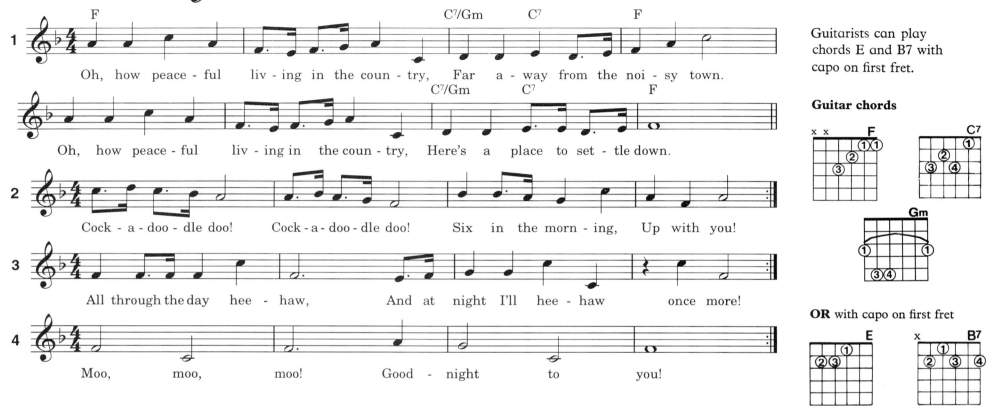

Words and music: Jan Holdstock

This round can be built up with each group singing only one part. Groups 2, 3 and 4 will need to sing their parts twice for each repetition of Group 1's part.

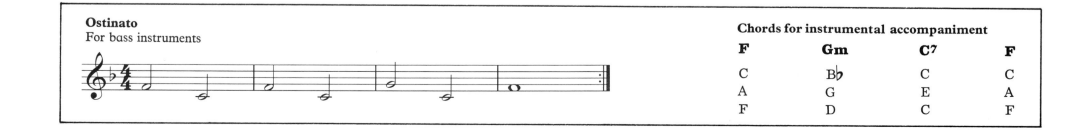

Ostinato
For bass instruments

Chords for instrumental accompaniment

F	Gm	C7	F
C	B♭	C	C
A	G	E	A
F	D	C	F

61 Christmas cake

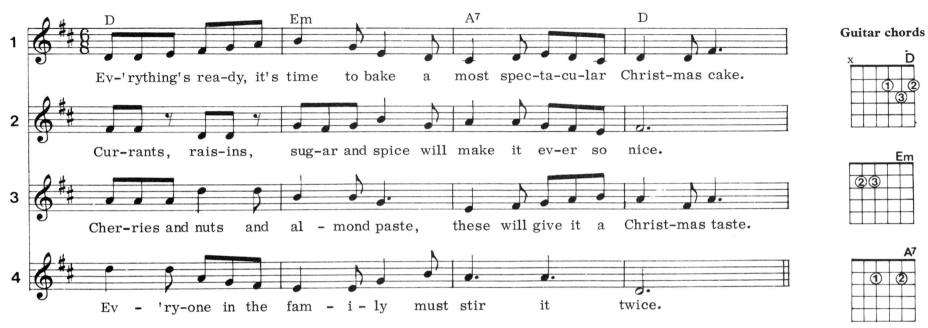

Guitar chords

1. Ev-'rything's rea-dy, it's time to bake a most spec-ta-cu-lar Christ-mas cake.
2. Cur-rants, rais-ins, sug-ar and spice will make it ev-er so nice.
3. Cher-ries and nuts and al - mond paste, these will give it a Christ-mas taste.
4. Ev - 'ry-one in the fam - i - ly must stir it twice.

Words and music: Jan Holdstock

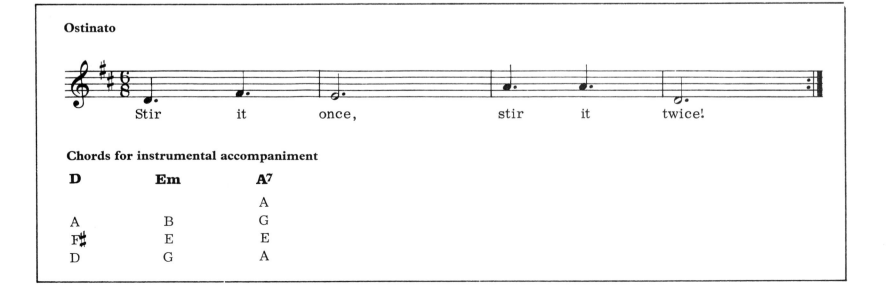

Ostinato

Stir it once, stir it twice!

Chords for instrumental accompaniment

D	Em	A⁷
		A
A	B	G
F♯	E	E
D	G	A

62 Come and sing together

1. If you'd dance, then you must have boots of shi-ning leath - er.
Mon - ey in your pock-et book, In your cap a feath - er.
But if you would sing with me, You don't need a
cent, you see. So come and sing to-geth - er!

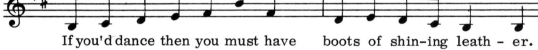

If you'd dance then you must have boots of shin-ing leath - er.

Guitar chords

Chords for instrumental accompaniment

Bm	D
B	
F♯	A
D	F♯
B	D

2 If you'd wed a pretty girl,
That will cost you money.
She will want a hundred things,
Rainy days or sunny.
But if you would sing with me,
You don't need a cent, you see.
So come and sing together!
If you'd wed a pretty girl,
That will cost you money.

3 If you want another verse,
(How could we be knowing?)
Why not make one up yourself,
Just to keep it going?
Music is for everyone,
You can have a lot of fun.
So come and sing together!
Try a verse you made yourself,
Then just keep it going.

Words and music: from a Hungarian folk round

This song can be sung as a two-part round, the second part beginning when the first part reaches*, or the beginning of the second bar.

63 Steeplejack

Briskly

1. "What do you call a
2. drun-ken It-al-ian steeple-jack?" "A
3. high tid-dl-y-I-ti."

Words and music: Ken Lee

The round is best sung unaccompanied once the parts can be put together.

Ostinato

This ostinato will be helpful in keeping the rhythm going, particularly during the rests of the last bar of the round.

Hi - tid-dl-y - hi - ti!   (clap) (clap)

64 Today I feel older

1. To - day I feel old-er,
2. than I ev-er felt in my life.
3. That's not surprising real-ly,
4. I am.

Words and music: Jan Holdstock

Ostinato
For bass instruments

The ostinato will be helpful in counting the rests while the song is being learnt. Sniffing for each silent beat is another way of counting the rests. When sung as a round, it is best done 'dead pan' without ostinato or sniffs.

Chords for instruments

Dm	A⁷
	A
A	G
F	E
D	C♯

Guitar chords

65 Rowdy round

This round can be sung by four independent groups of singers, one to each section, or as a regular round with the second part beginning when the first part reaches the second line.

Doo-dle doo! Doo-dle doo! Lis-ten while I sing to you. Now it's

I can sing mee-ow, mee-ow. I can sing mee-ow, mee-ow. I can

I shall go to-day, hee-haw, Sing-ing on my way, hee-haw,

I'll sing too, Bow-wow-wow like you.

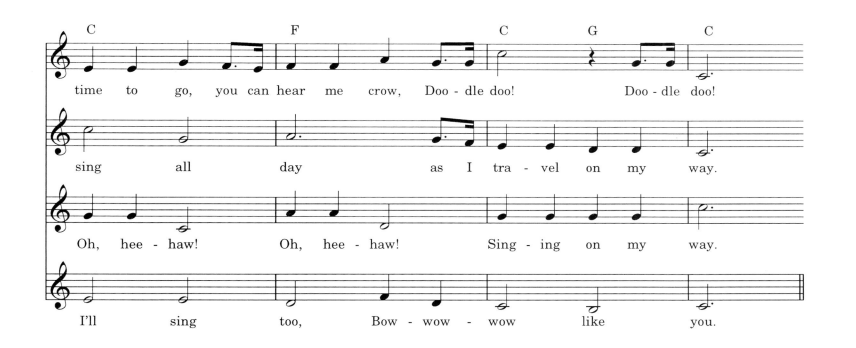

Guitar chords

Words and music: Jan Holdstock

Chords for instruments			
C	**F**	**D**	**G**
G	C	A	D
E	A	F♯	B
C	F	D	G

66 Happy Christmas

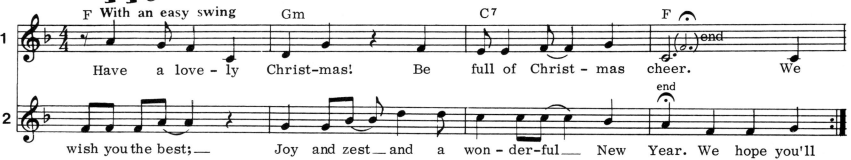

1 F With an easy swing   Gm   C⁷   F

Have a love-ly Christ-mas! Be full of Christ-mas cheer. We

2 wish you the best; — Joy and zest — and a won-der-ful — New Year. We hope you'll

Words and music: James Wild

Guitar chords

Ostinati

Hap - py Christ - mas! Hap-py Christ - mas! Hap-py Christmas to you. Yes, have a

Percussion

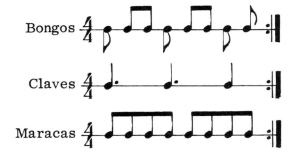

Bongos

Claves

Maracas

Chords for instrumental accompaniment

F	Gm	C⁷
		C
C	D	B♭
A	G	G
F	B♭	C

Build the round gradually so that each element in the music is heard separately as a 'solo spot' before being combined in the grand finale.

67 Noel, Noel!

1. No-el, No-el! No-el, No-el! No-el, No-el! No-el, No-el!

2. Jesus was born on Christmas day, — Long a-go and far a-way. —

3. Bells in the steep-le ring-ing clear — are wishing you a happy New Year.

Words and music: Jan Holdstock

The ostinati and chords given on the opposite page can also be used with "Noel, Noel".

PARTNER SONGS

The two rounds "Have a lovely Christmas" and "Noel, Noel" can be sung together as partner songs (track 67a).

68 Calypso

1. A-ny time you need a ca - lyp - so, here is what__ you must do.

2. First of all you need a rhy-thm, so shake a lit-tle, shake a lit-tle, shake a lit-tle sha-ker, and you

3. bang a drum__ and you sing and strum and then there's a ca-lyp - so for you.

Words and music: Jan Holdstock

Make up a simple dance to suit the words. It's often a good idea to dance to the song before attempting to sing in parts.

Guitar chords

Rhythms

shaker

bongos

(car-ni-val, car-ni-val, danc-ing)

claves

Chords for instruments

D	G	A⁷
		G
A	D	E
F♯	B	C♯
D	G	A

Ostinati

These ostinati are best played on a bass instrument.

(Need a rhy - thm, you need a rhy - thm, you .....)

The ostinato below uses the same notes as the one above, but has an easier rhythm:

69 Mrs O'Leary's lantern

Late last night, be - fore she went to bed,

Mis - sis O' - Lear - y hung a lan-tern in the shed and then a

cow kicked it o - ver and winked at her and said, "There'll be a

hot time in the old town to - night. Fire, Fire, Fire!"

Words and music: anonymous

Care will be needed in returning to the beginning of the tune after the off-beat "Fire! Fire! Fire!". If there is difficulty in keeping time, the singers might beat four beats in a bar throughout, or some might conduct while others sing.

Stopping this round can be a problem when all the parts are going. The leader can take a firm line (e.g. by clicking the fingers) to slow the music to a stop at the sign ⌢.

Guitarists can play chords E and B7 with capo on first fret.

Guitar chords

OR with capo on first fret

Chords for instrumental accompaniment	
F	**C⁷**
	B♭
C	G
A	E
F	C

70 Junkanoo

Junkanoo is a Jamaican Christmas festivity. Processions of merrymakers, masked dancers and drummers go through the streets, singing and playing fifes. The masks the dancers wear are often made to resemble the heads of cows and horses, and other characters like Bride and devil are mimed.

A processional dance can accompany the round, or the dance can be used as an interlude, with recorders playing the tune while the singers take a rest.

Words and music: Jan Holdstock

Ostinato

The ostinato is best played on a bass instrument. Open strings of the cello, or the double bass, would be good, or the bass guitar could be used.

Chords for instrumental accompaniment

G	**Am**	**D⁷**
		D
D	E	C
B	A	F♯
G	C	D

If chime bars are used for chordal accompaniment, it will be helpful to have another set of G chord bars for the last chord in each line.

Percussion

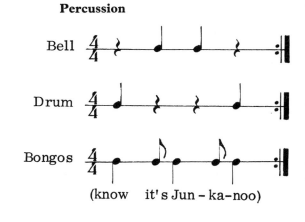

In an extended performance, the rhythm and instruments could be changed. See those suggested for "Calypso" (no. 68).

71 Old Bill Jones

1. Old Bill Jones lived in Hatchet Bay.— He walked in the most pe-cu-li-ar way.— He
2. had a wooden leg, A little wooden peg And as he walked— all the people would say,
3. Tramp, tramp, lis-ten to Bill,— Tramp, tramp, o-ver the hill.— You can
4. hear him go-ing tramp, tramp, with his little wooden leg.

Words and music: Jan Holdstock

PARTNER SONGS

The two songs "Junkanoo" and "Old Bill Jones" can be sung together as partner songs (track 71a).

Guitar chords

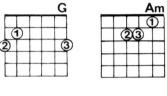

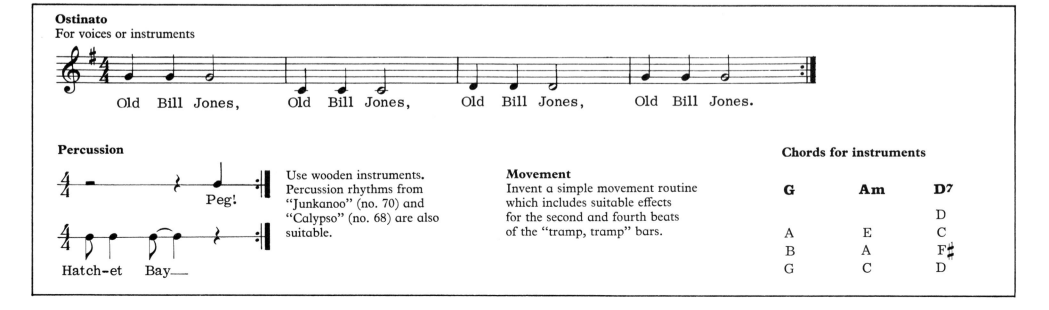

Ostinato
For voices or instruments

Old Bill Jones, Old Bill Jones, Old Bill Jones, Old Bill Jones.

Percussion

Peg!

Hatch-et Bay—

Use wooden instruments. Percussion rhythms from "Junkanoo" (no. 70) and "Calypso" (no. 68) are also suitable.

Movement
Invent a simple movement routine which includes suitable effects for the second and fourth beats of the "tramp, tramp" bars.

Chords for instruments

G	Am	D7
		D
A	E	C
B	A	F♯
G	C	D

72 Mr Rabbit

Mis-ter Rab-bit, Mis-ter Rab-bit, Your ears are might-y long.

Yes, my Lord, they're put on wrong. Ev - 'ry lit-tle soul must

shine, shine, shine. Ev - 'ry lit-tle soul must shine, (clap) shine, shine.

Words and music: anonymous

Guitar chord

Instrumental chord
F
C
A
F

This round can be sung in up to nine parts. Each new part comes in on the fourth beat of the bar.

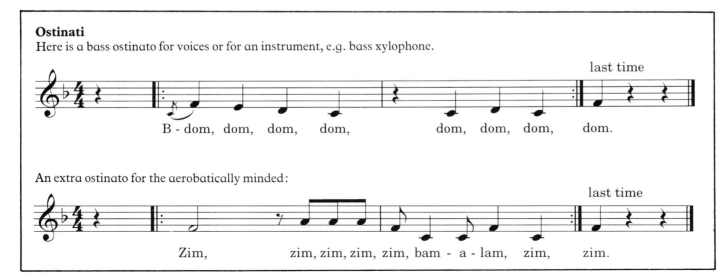

Ostinati

Here is a bass ostinato for voices or for an instrument, e.g. bass xylophone.

B - dom, dom, dom, dom, dom, dom, dom, dom.

An extra ostinato for the aerobatically minded:

Zim, zim, zim, zim, zim, bam - a - lam, zim, zim.

73 Fie, nay prithee, John

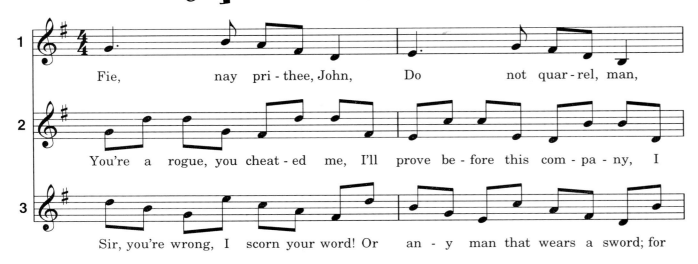

1. Fie, nay pri-thee, John, Do not quar-rel, man,

2. You're a rogue, you cheat-ed me, I'll prove be-fore this com-pa-ny, I

3. Sir, you're wrong, I scorn your word! Or an - y man that wears a sword; for

This song has a wide range from its highest to its lowest note and is full of jumps which need very careful pitching. Don't go too fast at first.

It is tremendous fun to sing when thoroughly learnt.

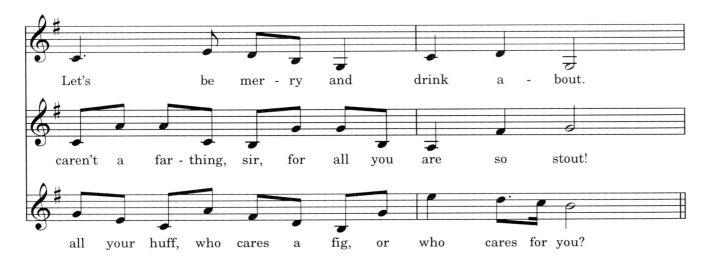

Let's be mer-ry and drink a - bout.

caren't a far-thing, sir, for all you are so stout!

all your huff, who cares a fig, or who cares for you?

Words and music: anonymous, from the early 18th century

74 Freedom train

1. This old free-dom train is such a long time in a-com-in', Now there's
2. none who can't af-ford it so you come and climb a-board it, Sing-in'
3. free — dom! Gonna have
4. free — dom! Gonna have
5. freedom! Free-dom! Free-dom!

Words and music: Ralph Alan Dale

Guitarists can play chords E, (A), E, (B7) with capo on first fret. The bracketed chords are not essential for unison singing.

Guitar chords

OR with capo on first fret

Be very careful that the rests are correctly learnt or there will be a derailment when the parts are put together.

When singing the round, begin with the ostinato only, very quietly, and build up the sound as the train gets nearer, then fade away again. A train whistle can be added at the climax, either a three-tone whistle or recorders with the body removed.

Ostinato
Use as an introduction and sustain throughout with one or several voices.

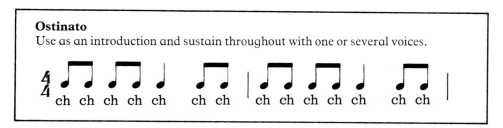
ch ch ch ch ch ch ch ch ch ch ch ch ch ch

75 Camel driver

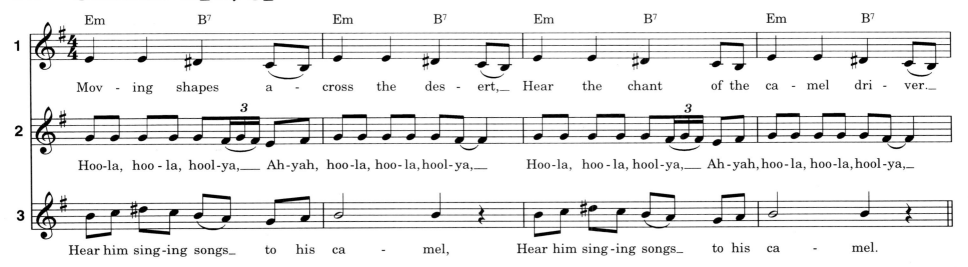

Part 1: Mov- ing shapes a - cross the des - ert,— Hear the chant of the ca - mel dri - ver.—

Part 2: Hoo-la, hoo - la, hool-ya,— Ah-yah, hoo-la, hoo-la, hool-ya,— Hoo-la, hoo - la, hool-ya,— Ah-yah, hoo-la, hoo-la, hool-ya,—

Part 3: Hear him sing-ing songs_ to his ca - mel, Hear him sing-ing songs_ to his ca - mel.

Words and music: Brian Fitzgerald

Like many rounds, this one doesn't want to stop. Try fading away, as though into the distance, each part dropping out as it comes to the end of the song.

Ostinato
Add exotic percussion to create a mysterious atmosphere, e.g.

Indian bells

Cymbal (not too loud)

Chords for instruments

Em	B7
	A
B	F♯
G	D♯
E	B

Guitar chords

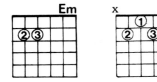

Em   x   B7

76 Zum gali gali

Guitar chords

Em

Am

1. Pi - o - neers must work ev - 'ry day From dawn till day is done; From dawn till day is done, There is work for ev - 'ry - one.

Zum ga - li ga - li ga - li, zum ga - li ga - li, Zum ga - li ga - li ga - li zum.

2 Pioneers will sing and dance,
   Dance the hora in a ring;
   Dance the hora in a ring,
   With their best girls dance and sing.
     Zum gali gali . . .

3 Pioneers will work for peace
   From dawn till day is done;
   From dawn till day is done,
   True peace for everyone.
     Zum gali gali . . .

Words and music: from an Israeli work song

Chords for instruments	
Em	**Am**
B	C
G	A
E	E

The chorus of this song can be sung by a second group as an introduction and as a second part all through the song.

77 A ram sam sam

78 Pease pudding hot

A ram sam sam, a ram sam sam, gu-li gu-li gu-li gu-li gu-li ram sam sam.

A ra-fi, a ra-fi, gu-li gu-li gu-li gu-li gu-li ram sam sam.

Words and music: traditional Israeli

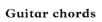

Guitar chords

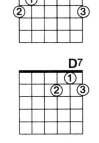

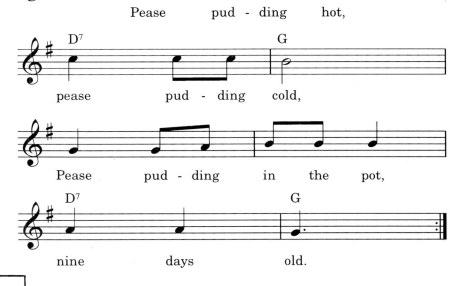

Pease pud-ding hot, pease pud-ding cold, Pease pud-ding in the pot, nine days old.

Words and music: traditional English

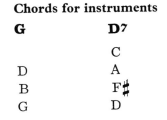

Chords for instruments

G	D⁷
	C
D	A
B	F♯
G	D

Ostinato

last time

Begin like this:

A ram sam sam, a ram sam sam, gu-li

Pease pud-ding hot,

PARTNER SONGS

Words and music: traditional American, adapted

Words and music: Jan Holdstock

Here are the words of both songs:

1 If you're happy and you know it, clap your hands (clap, clap)
   If you're happy and you know it, clap your hands (clap, clap)
   If you're happy and you know it, and you really want to show it,
   If you're happy and you know it, clap your hands (clap, clap)

2 If you're happy and you know it, stamp your feet (stamp, stamp)

3 If you're happy and you know it, hit a gong (gong, gong)

4 If you're happy and you know it, play a drum (drum, drum)

5 If you're happy and you know it, blow a horn (blow, blow)

6 If you're happy and you know it, tap two sticks (tap, tap)

7 If you're happy and you know it, shout "We are!" ("We are!")

1 If you clap (clap, clap) when you're feeling sad,
   If you clap (clap, clap) when you're feeling sad,
   Keep it steady (clap), don't hurry (clap)
   And you won't have time to worry (clap).

2 If you stamp (stamp, stamp) when you're feeling sad

3 If you gong (gong, gong) when you're feeling sad

4 If you drum (drum, drum) when you're feeling sad

5 If you blow (blow, blow) when you're feeling sad

6 If you tap (tap, tap) when you're feeling sad

7 If you shout (shout, shout) when you're feeling sad

These two songs are great fun to sing together, with the action/percussion alternating between the two. The melodies must be thoroughly learnt, and the rests carefully marked.

The words of verses 3 to 6 can be adapted to suit the resources available, or actions can be used in place of playing instruments. If instruments are being used as suggested above, it will help to subdivide each of the two large groups into four smaller ones, one with gongs or triangles, one with drums, one with wind instruments, and one with pairs of sticks or wood blocks. Everyone in each large group can sing all the words of their song, but, in verses 3 to 6, just the appropriate small group provides the action.

Chords for instruments

G	**D7**	**C**
	D	C
D	C	G
B	F♯	E
G	D	C

Guitar chords

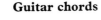

81 Winds through the olive trees

1 Winds through the olive trees
Softly did blow
Round little Bethlehem,
Long, long ago.

2 Sheep on the hillside lay
White as the snow;
Shepherds were watching them,
Long, long ago.

3 Then from the happy skies
Angels bent low,
Singing their songs of joy,
Long, long ago.

4 For in his manger bed,
Cradled we know,
Christ came to Bethlehem,
Long, long ago.

Words and music (81): from a traditional Gascon carol

82 O my little Augustin

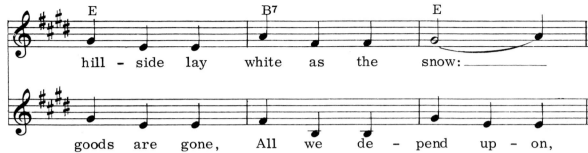

hill - side lay white as the snow:____

goods are gone, All we de - pend up - on,

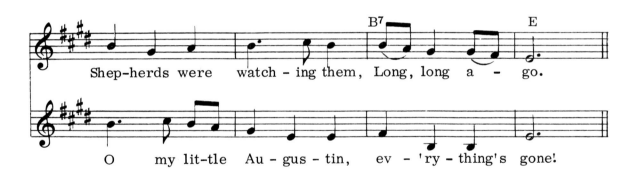

Shep-herds were watch - ing them, Long, long a - go.

O my lit-tle Au - gus - tin, ev - 'ry - thing's gone!

1 O my little Augustin,
Augustin, Augustin,
O my little Augustin,
Everything's gone.
Our money and goods are gone,
All we depend upon,
O my little Augustin,
Everything's gone.

2 O my little Augustin,
Augustin, Augustin,
O my little Augustin,
Everything's gone.
Our clothes are gone and our bags,
Augustin's dressed in rags.
O my little Augustin,
Everything's gone.

Chords for instruments

E	B⁷
	A
B	F♯
G♯	D♯
E	B

Guitar chords

E   x   B7

Words and music (82): from the traditional German

83 What shall we do with the drunken sailor ?

PARTNER SONGS

1 What shall we do with the drunken sailor,
What shall we do with the drunken sailor,
What shall we do with the drunken sailor,
Early in the morning ?
    Hooray and up she rises,
    Hooray and up she rises,
    Hooray and up she rises,
    Early in the morning.

2 Put him in the long boat until he's sober,
Put him in the long boat until he's sober,
Put him in the long boat until he's sober,
Early in the morning.
    Hooray and up she rises . . .

3 Pull out the plug and wet him all over,
Pull out the plug and wet him all over,
Pull out the plug and wet him all over,
Early in the morning.
    Hooray and up she rises . . .

4 Put him in the scuppers with a hosepipe on him,
Put him in the scuppers with a hosepipe on him,
Put him in the scuppers with a hosepipe on him,
Early in the morning.
    Hooray and up she rises . . .

Words and music (83): Sea shanty

84 O sinner man

O sinner man, where will you run to,
O sinner man, where will you run to,
O sinner man, where will you run to,
All on that day?

1 Run to the rocks, rocks won't you hide me?
Run to the rocks, rocks won't you hide me?
Run to the rocks, rocks won't you hide me?
All on that day.
  O sinner man . . .

2 Run to the sea, sea is a-boiling,
Run to the sea, sea is a-boiling,
Run to the sea, sea is a-boiling,
All on that day.
  O sinner man . . .

3 Run to the Lord, Lord won't you hide me?
Run to the Lord, Lord won't you hide me?
Run to the Lord, Lord won't you hide me?
All on that day.
  O sinner man . . .

4 O sinner man, should bin a-praying,
O sinner man, should bin a-praying,
O sinner man, should bin a-praying,
All on that day.
  O sinner man . . .

Words and music (84): Spiritual

Chords for instruments

Dm	C
A	G
F	E
D	C

Guitar chords

85 Down in Demerara

1. There was a man who had a hor-se-lum, had a hor-se-lum,

1. One at a time the hor - ses came, Trot - ting past the

1. Old wo - man, old wo - man, Are you fond of

had a hor-se-lum, Was a man who had a hor-se-lum, Down in De - me - ra - ra.

win - dow. One at a time the hor - ses came, Trot - ting through the door.

walk - ing? Speak a lit - tle loud - er, sir, I'm ra - ther hard of hear - ing.

The chorus of "Down in Demerara" can be sung also between the verses of the other songs.

Ostinato
For bass xylophone or other bass instrument

Chords for instruments	
F	**C**
	C
C	G
A	E
F	C

86 Trotting horses   87 Old woman

Down in Demerara

1 There was a man who had a horselum,
   Had a horselum, had a horselum,
   Was a man who had a horselum,
   Down in Demerara.
   And here we sits like birds in the wilderness,
   Birds in the wilderness, birds in the wilderness,
   Here we sits like birds in the wilderness,
   Down in Demerara.

2 Now that poor horse he broke a legalum,
   Broke a legalum, broke a legalum,
   That poor horse he broke a legalum,
   Down in Demerara.
   And here we sits . . .

3 Now that poor man he sent for a doctorum,
   Sent for a doctorum, sent for a doctorum,
   That poor man he sent for a doctorum,
   Down in Demerara.
   And here we sits . . .

4 Now that poor horse he went and diedalum,
   Went and diedalum, went and diedalum,
   That poor horse he went and diedalum,
   Down in Demerara.
   And here we sits . . .

5 And here we sits and flaps our wingsalum,
   Flaps our wingsalum, flaps our wingsalum,
   Here we sits and flaps our wingsalum,
   Down in Demerara.
   And here we sits . . .

Words and music: British student song

Trotting horses

1 One at a time the horses came,
   Trotting past the window,
   One at a time the horses came,
   Trotting through the door.

2 Two at a time the horses came,
   Trotting past the window,
   Two at a time the horses came,
   Trotting through the door.

3 Three at a time . . .

4 Four at a time . . .

5 Five at a time . . .

Words and music: Jan Holdstock

Game
The children form a circle with arms
up to make arches. One child trots
round the outside of the circle. At the
words "through the door", the child
goes in under one arch and out through
the next, i.e. round one of the children
in the circle. This child is the next
horse and joins the first child going
round the circle. Then the two of them
go in under one arch and out under
another, taking a third child with
them, and so on.

Guitar chords

OR with capo on first fret

Old woman

1 Old woman, old woman,
   Are you fond of walking?
   Speak a little louder, sir,
   I'm rather hard of hearing.

2 Old woman, old woman,
   Are you fond of talking?
   Speak a little louder, sir,
   I'm rather hard of hearing.

3 Old woman, old woman,
   Are you fond of cooking?
   Speak a little louder, sir,
   I'm rather hard of hearing.

4 Old woman, old woman,
   Are you fond of courting?
   Speak a little louder, sir,
   I think I almost heard you.

5 Old woman, old woman,
   Would you like to wed me?
   Lord have mercy on my soul
   But now I really hear you!

Words and music: traditional

88 Just for the record

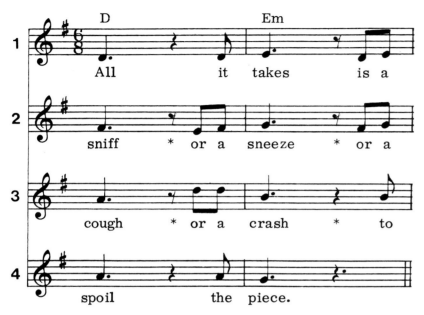

All it takes is a
sniff * or a sneeze * or a
cough * or a crash * to
spoil the piece.

Words and music: Jan Holdstock

Add appropriate noises at * until the music is obliterated!

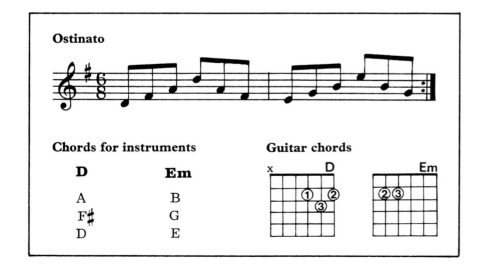

Ostinato

Chords for instruments

D	**Em**
A	B
F♯	G
D	E

Guitar chords

choo

Acknowledgements

Grateful thanks are due to those who helped in the development of this book, and in particular to the students of Bishop Grosseteste College, Lincoln; Jo and Tamsin Gadsby; Ralph Orlowski, Janet Poynton and Michelle Simpson. The publishers are also grateful James Wild and to SING FOR PLEASURE for allowing the inclusion of rounds composed by members of their organisation.

The following copyright owners have kindly granted their permission for the inclusion of music and words:

John Bannister for the words adaptation of 13 'Sing this song' and for the melody of 53 'Things that go bump in the night'.

Kate Baxter for the words of 2 'Music is fun'.

BBC Publications for the use of words by Michael Jessett in 13 'Sing this Song'.

Boosey & Hawkes Music Publishers Ltd for the melody of 42 'Old Abram Brown' from *Friday Afternoons*, Op.7 by Britten/Anon © 1936 by Boosey & Co Ltd.

Deborah C Burbridge for the melodies of 45 'Little wind' and 48 'The cold old house'.

Ralph Alan Dale for the melody and words of 20 'Trav'lin' round' and 74 'Freedom Train' from Music in the Round.

Brian Fitzgerald for the melody and words of 75 'The camel driver' © 1976 Brian Fitzgerald.

Jo Gadsby for the melody and words of 17 'Morning, Mr Blackbird' © 1981 Jo Gadsby.

Girl Guides Association of Victoria, Australia for 29 'Kookaburra' and 43 'I like the flowers' reprinted from the *Australian Campfire Song Book* by permission of the Girl Guides Association of Victoria.

Christopher Green for the words of 28 'On the river flows' and 41 'Bellringer, pray give us some peace'.

Beatrice Harrop for the words of 14 'Hey ho! Time to go to bed', 16 'Kite flying high, English adaptation of 25 'Ticking clocks', the music of 18 'Thirty purple birds', and the music of 37 'Hodge's grace'.

Harvard University Press for the words of 72 'Mister Rabbit' from *On the Trail of Negro Folk Songs* by Dorothy Scarborough © 1925 by Harvard University Press, 1953 by Mary McDaniel Parke and Mr Dowd of Charleston South Carolina.

John Hilton for the words and music of 46 'Come follow'.

Lovely Music, 17 Westgate, Tadcaster, N Yorks for the words and music of 33 'Clap, stamp, slap, click, 38 'Hard fact', 47 'Gravity', 57 'The Wreck', 60 'Country Life', 61 'Christmas cake', 64 'Today I feel older' (Lifelines 1); and 68 'Calypso'; for 59 'Sound waves', 67 'Noel Noel!' 88 'Just for the record' from *Choristers' Holiday*; and for 80 'If you clap' and 86 'Trotting horses', all by Jan Holdstock.

Ken Lee for the melodies of 4 'A thousand hairy savages' and 63 'Steeplejack'.

Spike Milligan for the words of 4 'A thousand hairy savages' from Silly Verse for Kids, Puffin Books and 52 'Baby Sardine' from *A Book of Milliganimals*, Puffin Books.

Novello & Company Ltd, 8/9 Frith Street, London W1V 5TZ for 5 'White Swans' from *A First Round Book* compiled and edited by Kenneth Simpson © copyright 1959 Novello & Company Limited, and 10 'Something inside me' from 77 *Rounds and Canons* compiled and edited by Kenneth Simpson © copyright 1980 Novello & Company Limited, and for the melody of 72 'Mister Rabbit' from English Songs for Children. Music compiled by Peggy Stake and arranged by Elizabeth Harding. All reproduced by permission of Novello & Company Limited, 8/9 Frith Street, London W1V 5TZ.

Oxford University Press for the words of 22 'Frogs' Festival'. Words translated by Mabel F Wilson from *Sing a Round* © Oxford University Press 1964 and for 40 'Blow the wind southerly'. Words and music by Imogen Holst from *Singing for Pleasure* © Oxford University Press 1957. Both used by permission.

Thomas Pitfield for the melody and words of 51 'Old Jim John'.

Roberton Publications for the melody of 50 'Poor Fly' from *Three Insect Songs* by Carey Blyton.

Jane Sebba for the melody of 26 'Water Wagtail'. The words were first published in *Poems from Bristol Schools*.

Sing for Pleasure for the melody of 1 'Algy' by Pat Shaw; the words and melody of 7 'Lollipop man' and 23 'Nice but naughty thoughts', both by John Coates; the melody of 52 'Baby sardine' by P Wooding/J Wild; the melody of 55 'To stop the train' by P Shaw/J Wild; the words and melody of 56 'The duchess' by Arthur Lucas; the words and melody of 66 'Happy Christmas' by James Wild; the words and melody of 70 'Junkanoo' and 71 'Old Bill Jones' both by Jan Holdstock.

Universal Edition (London) Ltd for the melody and words of 6 'Cuckoos gone away' from *Turnip Head* © 1980 by Universal Edition (London) Ltd, London and 65 'Rowdy Round' from *The Musicians of Bremen*, © 1981 Universal Edition (London) Ltd, London, both by Jan Holdstock. Reproduced by permission.

World Around Songs, Burnsville, NC for 12 'Donkeys and Carrots', English paraphrase by Augustus D Zanzig from *101 Rounds for Singing* published by World Around Songs, Inc and 58 'Let us sing together', adapted from a Czech folk tune by Max V Exner, from *Bridge of Song* © 1957 by Cooperative Recreation Service Inc. Transferred to World Around Songs, 1979. Used with permission.

The partner songs 77 and 78 'A ram sam sam' and 'Pease Pudding hot', 81 and 82 'Winds through the olive trees' and 'O my little Augustin', 83 and 84 'What shall we do with the drunken sailor?' and 'O sinner man', and 85 and 87 'Down in Demerara' and 'Old woman' are taken from *Mix 'n' Match* as published by **Universal Edition (London) Ltd**.

In spite of every effort, it has not been possible to trace the source of every round included. If any right has been omitted, the publishers offer their apologies and will rectify the omission in subsequent editions following notification.

CD recording:
Voices: Vivien Ellis, Kirsty Hoiles and Sam Kenyon
Guitar: Missak Takoushian
Accompaniments performed by Stephen Chadwick
Sound engineer: Stephen Chadwick

Index of first lines